You trail, 16–13, with a little more than a minute to go!

You have just scored and must now kick off. You have three time-outs remaining. What should you do on the kickoff? Should you attempt an onside kick—squirt the ball ten yards and try to recover it? Or should you kick deep and hope that a combination of tough defense and your three time-outs can get the ball back in time to score more points?

—To kick deep, turn to page 114.
—For an onside kick, turn to page 116.

REMEMBER—YOUR DECISIONS CAN PUT YOU IN THE SUPER BOWL!

PLAY IT YOUR WAY SPORTS BOOKS for you to enjoy

#1 *Can You Win the Pennant?*
#2 *Pro Football Showdown*

Available from ARCHWAY paperbacks

A Play-It-Your-Way
Sports Book #2

PRO FOOTBALL SHOWDOWN

Mitch Gelman

Illustrated by Al Fiorentino

AN ARCHWAY PAPERBACK
PUBLISHED BY POCKET BOOKS • NEW YORK

This novel is a work of fiction. Names, characters, places and incidents are either a product of the author's imagination or are used fictitiously. Any resemblance to actual events or locales or persons, living or dead, is entirely coincidental.

AN ARCHWAY PAPERBACK *Original*

 An Archway Paperback published by
POCKET BOOKS, a division of Simon & Schuster, Inc.
1230 Avenue of the Americas, New York, N.Y. 10020

ISBN: 0-671-46023-4

First Archway Paperback printing September, 1983

10 9 8 7 6 5 4 3 2 1

AN ARCHWAY PAPERBACK and colophon are trademarks of Simon & Schuster, Inc.

WHICH WAY is a registered trademark of Simon & Schuster, Inc.

PLAY IT YOUR WAY is a trademark of Simon & Schuster, Inc.

Printed in the U.S.A.

IL 4+

To Dad, Mom, Jan and all my
grandparents, some of whom
would have rather I called
signals from the sidelines,
but were proud I played.

ATTENTION!

Play-It-Your-Way Sports Books must be read in a special way. DO NOT READ THE PAGES IN ORDER. If you do, the story will make no sense at all. Instead, follow the directions at the bottom of each page until you come to an ending. Only then should you return to the beginning and start all over again, making different choices this time.

There are many possibilities for exciting football action. Some choices will lead your team to victory. Some choices will bring your team defeat. There are 25 different endings to this book—12 victories, 12 defeats and one surprise. Go back to the beginning as often as you like and try again. See how many times you can win.

Play alone or with a friend. And remember: follow the directions carefully. Good luck. Have fun!

You are the coach of the Warriors, one of the best teams in pro football. And one of the most surprising, too. At the beginning of the season, people laughed when you told them you had a good ball club. They thought you'd be lucky to win even half your games. But you knew better. And now, here you are, playing for the conference championship. This is the biggest game of your life. Your Warriors are playing the Gorillas—and the winner goes to the Super Bowl.

Five years ago, when you became coach, the Warriors were a terrible team. Most of the players were so old that sportswriters called the Warriors "The Museum for Prehistoric Ball Players." You were the laugh of the league.

You got rid of most of the old players and you began to build the team by drafting good, solid, college players. No prima donnas. No bonus babies with big salaries and no-cut contracts. You wanted players who would practice hard and play hard. Players who didn't think they knew it all. Players who would do things your way. You were looking to the future. Nothing could have been worse than the past.

(continued on page 2)

For a while, fans and sportswriters continued to laugh. They compared your young team to a nursery school class and asked you if you had nap time and milk and cookies during practice. But you knew in your head that this was the way to build a championship team. You knew that winning takes time.

Your first move was to draft Hungry Hank Hartman, a six-foot-four-inch 220-pound middle linebacker. He was given his nickname Hungry Hank because he once ate ten Giant-burgers and three Superburritos for a snack. And after watching films of his college games, you knew Hungry Hank also had an appetite for quarterbacks.

This season was Hank's best. Every time you looked up, he was making a key tackle, either stopping a runner just short of a first down or blitzing a quarterback to smithereens. "Hank is our leader out there," Ron Leonard, your All-Pro safety, has said. "He makes us get out there and hang tough even when we can't move another muscle."

(continued on page 3)

That's how you made it to this championship game—by hanging tough. Late in the fourth quarter, when the other teams begin to droop from fatique, your guys play their hardest. The whole season has been like that. The Warriors didn't win many games early in the year, but late in the season, when other teams were wearing out, your ball club seemed to get stronger. You won your last three games and squeezed into the play-offs. Then you began knocking off the so-called better teams.

Everybody thought your late-season surge was a fluke. But that is the way you planned it all along. That is why you made this season's summer training camp the toughest ever. "It's mind over matter," you told your players, as sweat poured off their faces the first day of training camp. "I don't mind and you don't matter. Remember, gentlemen, you hate me now, but you are going to love me when the play-offs start." And Clown Kennedy, the big defensive end who was a rookie at your very first Warrior training camp years ago, said "You tell us that every year, coach, and we ain't made the play-offs yet."

(continued on page 4)

Clown is the only player you let get away with wisecracks like that. That's because he's always in shape, never breaks training and, even when you're behind 60–0, he never gives up. The Clown may joke around in the locker room, but on the field he is all serious business. This season Clown led the league in quarterback sacks, getting one in almost every game. Everyone roots for Clown because after every game in which he sacks a quarterback twenty local supermarkets give away free sacks of groceries.

Led by the Clown, Hungry Hank and Ron Leonard, your defense was the best in the league. That defensive unit sure lived up to its nickname, "The Hit Men." But you had ex-

(continued on page 5)

pected the Hit Men to play well. The real surprise was your offense and that great second-year quarterback whom nobody else wanted, Tom Burns.

Tom came to the Warriors from a small college. Even though his college team was undefeated his junior and senior years, nobody seemed to notice. Most pro scouts had never heard of him and the ones who knew about him thought his arm wasn't strong enough for him to succeed in the National Football League. But you were at his last college game, and you liked what you saw: a quiet, cooperative quarterback who wasn't fancy, but who made no mistakes and had proven over the years that he knew how to win.

(continued on page 6)

You drafted Tom on the sixth round and this season he's proven he can win in the pros, too.

Your star running back, Whiz Wilson, is nothing like Tom. And nothing like any other player on your team, either. You like your players to work as a team and never boast about themselves. But Whiz has an ego so big that he won't put his helmet on until right before the first play of the game. "I don't want the fans to miss my pretty face," he says. He also says that "some day a shoe company is going to name a pair of sneakers after me, going to call them 'Whizzers.'"

Whiz is a rookie who won the Heisman Trophy in college. Despite his loud mouth, you drafted him because he had the backfield speed you needed to turn the Warriors into champions. He was the missing link. And this season he gained 1574 yards, with 18 touchdowns, for you, including a 67-yard end sweep for the winning touchdown in the first play-off game.

The second play-off game was last Sunday. You won it when Clown Kennedy recovered a fumble and, two plays later, Tom Burns threw a touchdown pass to Tiny Todd Lewis, the five-foot-six wide receiver the fans call "Super-midget." And now you're ready to start game three of the play-offs—against the Gorillas.

(continued on page 7)

The Gorillas have won four of the last six Super Bowls. They have an All-Pro fullback, Roger Walsh, who has not been stopped for a loss in three years. He just plods forward behind that big Gorilla line and pounds out the yards. They have super flanker, Elmers Kauffman. Elmers is not his real name, but everybody calls him that because his hands are like glue. Hardly ever drops a pass. And they have quarterback, Frank Ellis, who has been around so long and won so many big games that nothing worries him anymore. The other day a reporter asked Frank how nervous he gets before championship games. "Oh," said Frank, "about as nervous as when I brush my teeth."

Finally, there is the Gorilla whom opposing players fear the most—linebacker Killer Tedesco. The only real joy Killer gets out of life, he once told a reporter, is hearing a quarterback's ribs crack. Killer is the favorite of the Gorilla fans. And no wonder. Gorilla fans are the loudest, nastiest and rudest fans in all of football. Some of them come to games dressed in Gorilla costumes and throw bananas at the visiting team. The fans are so bad that opposing players and coaches call the Gorillas' stadium "The Zoo."

(continued on page 8)

And you've got to face those fans today. To go to the Super Bowl, you've got to win in The Zoo.

"Forget about the fans," you told your players in the locker room a while ago. "Don't let them get to you."

"Okay, coach," Clown Kennedy yelled from the back of the room. "But I hope they throw a lot of bananas 'cause I brought my Rice Krispies."

Everyone laughed. Clown is good for that. He knows how to break the tension at the right time. And, as always, his was the first name in your mind when you picked your starting players:

TODAY'S STARTERS

	Defense		Offense
LE	Clown Kennedy	WR	Tiny Todd Lewis
LT	Albert Farmer	LT	Leopold Jones
RT	Jonathan Culp	LG	Sam Kurtz
RE	Jackson Orlando	C	Arnie Hodge
LLB	Abdul Amat	RG	Curly Johanson
MLB	Hungry Hank Hartman	RT	Pete Caparelli
RLB	Frankie Rivers	TE	Ed Rosen
LCB	Yo Yo Carpenter	WR	R. J. King
RCB	Nathaniel Busby	QB	Tom Burns
FS	Ron Leonard	HB	Whiz Wilson
SS	Bobby Sam Smith	FB	Country Boone

(continued on page 9)

You've also got a great suicide squad, those guys who run down to cover the kickoff. And because of them, you're now facing your first big decision of the day. You have won the coin toss and must decide whether to kick or receive the ball to start the game. Most teams want to receive the ball, want the ball kicked to them. But many times this season, when you've kicked off, your suicide squad has stormed down and caused a fumble, setting you up with great early field position deep in your opponent's territory.

Should you receive the kickoff and have faith that your team can start a long, slow, touchdown drive? Or should you choose to kick off? Traditional football strategy goes against kicking off, but it might be worth the gamble. Your suicide squad could cause a fumble and put you in position to score quickly.

—*If you elect to receive, turn to page 10.*

—*If you choose to kick off, turn to page 22.*

The Gorillas kick high and long to your four-yard line. Yo Yo Carpenter catches the ball and speeds straight up the middle. With blockers in front of him, he shoots past the ten-yard line, the twenty. And suddenly he is hit head-on, a Gorilla tackler ramming his helmet into Yo Yo's stomach. For a moment, Yo Yo doesn't get up. He seems to be hurt. Oh, no. What a loss that would be! Yo Yo not only is your best man at returning kicks, he's also your best cornerback on defense. Those Gorillas are something. Always hurting somebody. Yo Yo had better be okay. Or you're in big trouble.

(continued on page 11)

Yo Yo leaps to his feet. "They only knocked the wind out of me, coach," he says. He's all right.

Now, you signal to quarterback Tom Burns. As the offense runs on the field, Tom stays back for a moment, talking to you. On some teams, the quarterback calls the plays. Not on the Warriors. You call the plays—all of them. And now you have to decide which one to use to start the game.

The first play is always important. It helps set the tone. Usually, you start with something conservative, something that just gets the game in motion and pits your power right up against the other team's. You can do that now. You can call a run up the middle.

Or you can gamble. Throw the bomb—a long pass downfield. A bomb on the first play might really shake up the Gorillas. You might even get a quick touchdown. They sure won't be expecting it because that's not your usual style.

But, of course, you'd be taking a risk. A long pass might be intercepted and that would really fire up the Gorillas and their crazy fans.

—If you call for a long pass, turn to page 12.

—If you call a running play, turn to page 38.

"Throw the bomb," you tell quarterback Burns. "Maybe we'll catch them sleeping."

Burns runs out to the huddle and calls the play. "Supermidget," he says to Tiny Todd Lewis, "you keep running and I'll get the ball to you."

With the center snap, Tiny Todd takes off and Burns fades back. Tiny Todd races downfield, crossing the 50-yard line as Burns lets the ball go. It's a good pass, high and far, a long, tight spiral. As the ball flies toward him, Tiny Todd spots it over his shoulder and reaches up.

(continued on page 13)

And can't quite get his hands on it. The ball was thrown just a bit too far. It falls to the ground. An incomplete pass.

But the Gorillas are shaken up. They were caught by surprise. They aren't sure what you're going to do now. The Warriors are known as a team that doesn't take big chances. But you took one on the very first play. The Gorillas have to be wondering now whether you've got a lot of surprises in store for them.

The Gorillas spread their defense a little bit to protect against another surprise pass. And you call a perfect play—a draw. Quarterback Burns drops back as if to pass, then suddenly slaps the ball into the belly of your big fullback, Country Boone. Country rambles right up the middle for 18 yards.

Mixing passes and runs, you drive into Gorilla territory. You get to the Gorilla 17-yard line now, third down with four yards to go for a first down. Do you call a short pass or a pitch-out to Whiz Wilson for a power sweep?

—To pitch out, turn to page 14.

—To throw a short pass, turn to page 18.

You send in your plays with your wide receivers. Tiny Todd and Charlie Baggett take turns. Tiny will go into the game for one down, then Charlie will replace him. Now it's Charlie's turn to carry the play in to the quarterback and stay in the game. You tell him the play: "Power toss, sweep right to the wide side of the field."

Charlie runs in and gives Tom Burns the instructions. This has been a terrific play for you all year. It sends Whiz racing wide around end, to the side of the field where there's a lot of room. Almost always, he's able to pick up short yardage on the play. And when he gets a good block downfield and is able to pick up a half-step on the cornerback, Whiz has the speed to turn the play into a touchdown.

At the line of scrimmage, Burns calls signals, steps back and pitches the ball to Whiz, who is in motion racing to the right side. With guard Curly Johanson in front of him, blocking, Whiz circles right end. Whiz and Curly have great teamwork. Whiz doesn't outrun him even though he has great speed. He follows the blocker as long as he can.

(continued on page 16)

Whiz and Curly are good friends off the field, too. They like to kid around in the locker room and pose for pictures together. They think it's real funny to pose for the pictures because Whiz has this great head of hair and Curly is stark bald. That's why the ballplayers gave him the nickname Curly.

Now Curly throws a strong block, springing Whiz for four yards. Charlie Baggett comes across and throws a good block, too, enabling Whiz to pick up three more yards. You're always happy when Charlie is in at wide receiver on these running plays. He's a much better blocker than Tiny Todd. "You are one great pass-catcher," Country Boone once told Tiny. "But you block about as well as those mosquitoes that used to try to eat my arm back home on the farm."

The power sweep has gained seven yards. Next, you call a pass to tight end Ed Rosen. Tom Burns fakes another pitch to Whiz Wilson, then lofts the ball into the corner of the end zone. Touchdown! And when Chub Kowalski kicks the extra point, you're ahead, 7–0.

(continued on page 17)

You hold the 7–0 lead through the first half. But the Gorillas come back strong in the second half. They take the kickoff and play after play they gain ground by running off right guard. Quickly, they tie the game. Suddenly, they're just mowing you down.

You know that the Gorillas have spotted some weakness in your defense. Maybe you should change some strategy. You've been playing a four-three defense—four linemen and three linebackers. That's what has worked for you all year. But maybe you should shift to a three-four—three linemen and four linebackers. With an extra linebacker, you'll give up something on your pass rush, but you'll have better pass coverage and better pursuit of runners. You've used the four-three with great success all year. You hate to panic and change now. Still, the Gorillas just ran right through you out there.

—If you switch to a three-four defense, turn to page 24.

—If you stick with your four-three defense, turn to page 28.

In the pocket, surrounded by his blockers, Tom Burns watches Tight End Ed Rosen cut across the middle. It is a slant-in pass, a play that has been very successful for the Warriors throughout the season. But not this time. Burns tries to fire the ball between the linebackers, but Killer Tedesco reaches up and slaps the ball down. Then the Killer goes into one of his routines that drives opponents crazy. He points at the Warriors, then thumps his chest with both fists, like a gorilla. His fans in the Zoo go wild. They stomp and thump and scream. Bananas pour onto the field.

(continued on page 19)

On fourth down, Chub Kowalski misses a field goal. The Gorillas take over and your defensive players, The Hit Men, hold. Forcing the Gorillas to punt, the Warriors get the ball on their own 33. As Tom Burns straps up his helmet, you tell him, "Sweep for Wilson. Let's try to break him loose."

From the bench you watch Whiz Wilson take the handoff and fly toward the sidelines. In an instant, he turns the corner and is heading downfield. "Break it, Whiz," you're yelling. "Break it."

You watch Whiz come up to a linebacker. The linebacker moves right and Whiz throws a hip at him, and a head fake. The linebacker dives in for a tackle. Reaching for Whiz, all the linebacker grabs is air.

"One more man, Whiz," you yell. "One more man to beat."

The man is Gorilla defensive back Timmy Wall. He's one of the fastest men in football. And he's bearing in on Whiz Wilson right now.

(continued on page 20)

Whiz fakes with his hip again. And with his head. Timmy Wall isn't fooled. He keeps bearing in and there's only one way for Whiz to beat him. With speed.

Whiz turns it on. Oh, man, does he turn it on. You've never seen him move so fast. He gets a half-step lead on Timmy Wall. And that's it. When Whiz has a lead, there's no player anywhere who can catch him. You see Whiz point his foot to the end zone with a little kick. Whenever he does that, you know he's home free. "All the way, Whizzer," you scream. "All the way." Ahead of Timmy Wall by two full steps now, Whiz Wilson charges into the end zone for a touchdown. A 67-yard touchdown run.

(continued on page 21)

Chub Kowalski kicks the extra point. The scoreboard flashes your lead, 7–0. And the Gorilla fans are suddenly very quiet.

During the time-out for television to show commercials, you think about your next move. The Gorillas have the best kick-returner in pro football, Lucifer Brown. Already this season Lucifer has returned six kickoffs for touchdowns. Do you risk kicking the ball deep down the middle where he's positioned? Or do you kick shorter and to one of the sidelines?

By kicking the ball up the middle, you give Chub Kowalski the chance to really drive the ball as high and as hard as he can, possibly driving it out of the end zone. But then again Lucifer Brown may be able to grab it and break loose.

By kicking the ball shorter and to the sidelines, you keep it away from Lucifer. But it could go out of bounds, bringing you a penalty. And if it stays in bounds, your suicide squad might not be able to get downfield and cover the kick effectively.

—If you kick the ball down the middle, turn to page 32.

—If you kick the ball away from Lucifer, turn to page 36.

Chub Kowalski, your kicker, tees up the ball on your 35-yard line. Then he boots it high in the air. It sails end over end to the Gorillas' two-yard line. Their speedy kick-returner, Lucifer Brown, catches it and bolts up the middle.

This is the way Lucifer starts most of his long kickoff returns—by running right up the middle behind a wedge of blockers, then bolting through an opening and breaking free to the outside. Once he gets to the outside, he is often impossible to stop.

So you know that the best way to stop him is to bust through the wedge. And you have just the guy who can do it. Byron Lebow. The Hatchet.

The Hatchet is six-two, 245 pounds and crazy. Before games he fires himself up by banging his helmet against the lockers. With his head in it.

The Hatchet is the best wedge-breaker you've ever coached. He doesn't worry about getting hurt. You watch him now as he storms downfield, throws his body to the ground and rolls into the wedge like a human bowling ball. As The Hatchet drives the blockers out of the way, two Warriors smash into Lucifer Brown and the ball pops loose. A fumble. Fadeaway Wallace, one of the stars of your suicide squad, falls on the ball.

(continued on page 23)

Your strategy worked. You have the ball on the Gorillas' 14-yard line. With a wonderful chance to go right in for a touchdown and shake them up so badly they may not recover.

All week your scouts have been telling you that there is one play that will catch the Gorillas completely by surprise, that will fool them so badly it will be an instant touchdown. What a great way that would be to start the game: recovered fumble, instant touchdown.

But it's a dangerous play—a quarterback keeper. The idea is for the quarterback to fake a handoff, then to hide the ball on his hip and, while everyone is moving to the left, sneak around right end. You've never used it before. The Gorillas would never expect it.

On the Warriors, the quarterback doesn't call the plays. You call them. But should you call this one? The danger is that quarterback Tom Burns could get tackled very hard. And if Tom Burns got hurt, you'd have almost no chance of winning the game.

—*To call a safer play, turn to page 62.*

—*To call the "quarterback keeper," turn to page 70.*

You tell your defensive coach, "Switch to the three-four." He nods and sends in Lionel Archer, a linebacker, to replace tackle Jonathan Culp. Moving out of their huddle, the Gorillas line up. Frank Ellis, their smart, veteran quarterback, looks over the defense and spots the change. Instantly, he switches his own play. You hear him call out an audible—a play change at the line of scrimmage.

You clench your fists. Sure is tough to try to fool Ellis. No matter what you try, he's seen it before. You kick at the ground and hold your breath.

Ellis fades back with the ball. He sets up. He looks downfield. His wide receivers have gone long, deep down the field. He fakes throwing long, then pulls the ball back in. With only three men on your defensive line, the Gorilla blockers are having an easy time stopping the pass rush. Ellis has all the time in the world. And that is dangerous.

(continued on page 25)

Downfield, Elmers Kauffman, the glue-fingered receiver, suddenly stops. He turns and comes back, shooting into an empty spot between your linebackers and defensive backs. That's the danger in giving a quarterback so much time. His receivers can maneuver around and eventually break free.

Instantly, Ellis fires. Complete to Kauffman. Twenty-five-yard gain.

Two more completions by Ellis move the ball to your 22-yard line. The Gorillas are hot. What do you do to stop them? Against your regular defense, they run for yardage. Against this one, they pass for yardage.

(continued on page 26)

Perhaps you should call a "blitz," have one of your linebackers shoot through the line of scrimmage at the snap of the ball. That would put pressure on the quarterback. That would take away his time. Maybe you'd even tackle him for a big loss.

But this is Frank Ellis, the most experienced quarterback around. Maybe he'll anticipate the blitz and take advantage of it. Maybe he'll be able to capitalize for an instant touchdown. Maybe you should just fake a blitz and stay in your three-four defense.

It's a war of wits between you and Frank Ellis. What do you do?

—To blitz, turn to page 35.

—To stay in your three-four, turn to page 40.

You're going to go with the fake and try to win the game right here. Country Boone takes the snap and bolts up the middle. He runs smack into Killer Tedesco. Country is one of the few backs in football strong enough to break one of Killer's tackles. But not this time. Killer wrestles him to the ground the way Country Boone himself hauls down steers when he rides in the rodeo.

The Gorillas have stopped you short of a first down. They control the ball a while, then punt to you deep in your own territory. By faking instead of punting, you sacrificed field position. You would have been better off pinning the Gorillas deep in their territory.

Now you're the ones pinned down. You're on your own ten-yard line. You have too far to go and too little time to get there. You start to move, but the clock runs out. You lose, 14–10.

The End

Your defense has been doing the job for you all year. You're not about to change it now. But you do make an adjustment. You tell your left linebacker, Abdul Amat, to start filling the gap because they're blowing in over right guard. Up to now, Abdul has been following your game plan and sliding to the outside in order to be in position to cut off sweeps and quick slant-out passes. But now you change your plan and Abdul does his job. He fakes sliding outside, then slips back into the hole. With a WHOMP! that can be heard in the stands, he smashes down Gorilla fullback Roger Walsh.

Next, Gorilla quarterback Frank Ellis tries to counter your strategy. He calls for play-action, sending Walsh into the hole, but without the ball. As Walsh heads for the hole and Abdul slides inside to stop him, Ellis looks to the outside, setting to throw into the flat that Abdul was vacating. But before Ellis can even lift his arm, Clown Kennedy tackles him from behind. Ellis is flat on his face in an instant, with Kennedy on top of him. A sack. There'll be some free groceries tomorrow.

(continued on page 30)

The score is still 7–7 at the end of three quarters. But the Gorillas get a field goal early in the fourth quarter to lead, 10–7. Late in the fourth quarter, you begin to move. With 26 seconds left in the game, you are behind 10–7 and have the ball on the Gorilla five-yard line.

It is third down and goal to go. You have two time-outs left. You use one now and call quarterback Burns to the sidelines. You tell him you're going to try for a field goal right now. "We'll get the three points, tie it up and win in overtime," you say. By trying the field goal now, on third down, you won't be risking a fumble or interception. Also, if you make a mistake, even if the ball is blocked and you recover it, you'll get another chance on fourth down.

"Wait a second, coach," Burns says. "I've got a better idea."

You can't believe what you're hearing.

(continued on page 31)

This is the first time your young quarterback has ever questioned one of your decisions. You listen, shocked.

Burns tells you that the Gorillas' left cornerback has been playing in tight for the run all game. And that, because of it, Tiny Todd can get open on a Z-out into the end zone off a play fake. "Here's what I want to do, coach," the young quarterback says. "We run a fake run off right tackle to draw the cornerback in. Tiny lines up, takes a step in as if to block on a running play. Then he shoots into the corner and I hit him for a touchdown. It'll work, coach. I *know* it will work."

—If you listen to your young quarterback turn to page 43.

—If you stick with your own strategy, turn to page 44.

You're not afraid. Lucifer is good. But so is your Suicide Squad. Your Suicide Squad is the best in the league. You have confidence in those guys.

Chub Kowalski booms the kick deep down the middle. Lucifer grabs it on his own three. He starts left, cuts right. And runs smack into the man you call The Hatchet. He's Byron Lebow, once a starting offensive guard, but now almost exclusively on the Suicide Squad. As an offensive guard, Byron had a reputation as one of the dirtiest players in the league. His temper would get him in lots of trouble. He would lose his head and mess up plays. The Suicide Squad is the perfect place for him. He can run straight down the field, busting people apart. Very little strategy for him to mess up. You just send old Byron straight ahead and let him hit people.

Now he drops Lucifer on the Gorilla 16-yard line. "Way to go, Hatchet," you yell.

(continued on page 33)

Your defense stops the Gorillas. After a punt, you get the ball in great field position on the Gorilla 49. You don't score, but you keep the Gorillas in their own territory throughout the first quarter. Then, on the first play of the second quarter, Burns finds R. J. King free deep downfield and passes to him for a touchdown. The Gorillas come back with a field goal, then Chub Kowalski kicks one for you. You go to the locker room at the end of the half, winning 17–3. You're dominating the game. You realize that the Gorillas can't stop you. The only thing that can stop you would be dumb mistakes by your own team.

(continued on page 34)

The Gorillas take the second-half kickoff and you stop Lucifer on the 21. Then your Hit Men stop two running plays. It's third down and nine yards to go for the Gorillas. You know it has to be a pass. Signaling from the sidelines, you send Bobby Sam Smith in on a safety blitz. And he roughs the passer.

The penalty gives the Gorillas a first down. And it gives them momentum. They score a touchdown. Then, in the fourth quarter, when their tight end slips in behind Bobby Sam, Ellis passes for another Gorilla touchdown.

You want two things. You want to strangle Bobby Sam. And you want to get the momentum back. The score is tied at 17, with five minutes to go. The Gorillas are kicking off. And your Warriors look asleep out there.

How can you wake them up? One way might be to call for a reverse kickoff return—to have one of your deep backs catch the ball, then hand it off to the other. Normally, you don't like that razzle-dazzle because you risk fumbling. Normally, you have faith that after a regular kickoff return, your offense will generate a long, scoring drive. Yet, you do need some momentum now.

—For a reverse kickoff return, turn to page 46.

—For a regular kickoff return, turn to page 50.

Hungry Hank Hartman gets ready to blitz. You know that he's telling his teammates what he always does in these situations. He's telling them: "I can taste that quarterback right now."

Hank crouches and, with the snap of the ball, charges in. Ellis is dropping back to pass and Hank is coming right at him. It looks like a great move! Then you realize your whole defensive line is getting in on Ellis and that his whole offensive line has formed a wall of blockers out front. He's outsmarted you. He's called a screen pass, where he lets your defenders rush in on him, then dumps the ball to a back behind a wall of blockers.

Ellis throws to Roger Walsh. And Walsh plods into the end zone behind the blockers. The Gorillas lead, 14–7.

Your defense is demoralized. And your offense can't move the ball. The Gorillas score two more touchdowns. You get none.

After the blitz that backfired, nothing works for you. You gambled and you lost, 28–7.

The End

You tell Chub Kowalski to kick the ball short, to the sidelines. He does and the ball bounces out of bounds. You're penalized five yards and he kicks again, this time from the 30-yard line. Lucifer Brown rushes in and grabs this kick, returning it all the way to the Gorilla 45. With Frank Ellis mixing runs up the middle with passes to the sidelines, the Gorillas drive for a touchdown. The score is tied, 7–7.

The Gorillas kick off, stop you, then block your punt and recover on your four-yard line. The reason the punt was blocked was because yesterday Martin Delacruz, your punter, twisted his left ankle in the shower. He kicks with his right foot, but the injury nevertheless has thrown him off stride. It has messed up his timing.

The Gorillas score again and lead 14–7 when the first half ends. Ten minutes into the third quarter, you get a field goal to make it 14–10. Now, with six minutes to go in the game, you have the ball at midfield and you have a big decision to make.

(continued on page 37)

It's fourth down and you're five yards from a first down. Normally, you'd have Delacruz punt into the coffin corner; then you'd rely upon your defense to hold the Gorillas and put you in good field position for a final touchdown drive. But with the injury, Delacruz might have another punt blocked. And if that happened, you'd be in big trouble.

Do you take a chance and let him punt?

Or do you take a chance on something else— a fake punt, with the center snapping the ball directly to the blocking back, Country Boone, who would then try to run for a first down.

—*If you call for a fake punt, turn to page 27.*

—*If you call for a punt, turn to page 52.*

You stand at the sidelines, watching your team in the huddle. Suddenly, you hear screams behind you—shrieking, bloodcurdling screams. Screams of young women who are really afraid of something.

You wheel around. Oh, no. Some of the crazy fans wearing Gorilla costumes have sneaked onto the field and captured two of the Warrior cheerleaders. Somehow, they have made it past the security guards and they are carrying the cheerleaders up into the stands. And one of those cheerleaders is your sister.

(continued on page 39)

"Help!" your sister is screaming. "Somebody help me!" She is terrified. You know that.

"Help me," she screams. And she calls out your name.

Without thinking, you leap over the bench and run to the stands. You push past two security guards. You pound up the stairs, throwing punches at anything in your way. You punch one man. Then another. Then a third.

And then, someone punches back. It is a roundhouse right that catches you square on the jaw. You fall backward and crack your head on the ground.

Perhaps the Warriors will win this game. But you won't find out for hours. You have been knocked unconscious and are on your way to the hospital on a stretcher.

The End

Hungry Hank Hartman stutters into the gap, moving as if he's about to blitz. But he's not going to blitz. He's only faking. It's a great fake, so great that the Gorillas' left guard, completely fooled, jumps offside. Hank's slick move has brought on a very important penalty against the Gorillas.

The penalty stops the Gorillas' momentum. They have to settle for a field goal. They go ahead, 10–7, but that's not bad, considering the way they were rolling.

Your team settles down now. You trail 10–7 as the third quarter ends and you're happy with the way things look. Behind by only three points, you're going into the fourth quarter. And that's been the quarter in which the Warriors have always been at their best.

The Gorillas stop you twice. You stop them once, and now, with eight minutes to go in the game, they have the ball again and run off three first downs. But your three-four defense cuts down two Gorilla runs. And it's third down, a passing situation.

(continued on page 41)

Frank Ellis drops back, looking for receivers. Clown Kennedy squirts through the blocks and puts on some pressure. With Clown coming at him, Ellis rushes his pass, trying to force it between two of your defensive backs, Nathaniel Busby and Ron Leonard. Busby tips the ball in the air and, just like in the drill your defensive backs practice every day, Leonard reaches up and snags it for an interception.

(continued to page 42)

The Gorilla fans sit silently for a minute. Then they begin waving their yellow- and black pennants and screaming for their team to stop you.

You have the ball on your own 35-yard line, with six minutes to go. You need a field goal to tie and a touchdown to win.

Whiz Wilson carries for nine yards. The pressure is really on now, and that's the way Whiz likes it. That's when he's at his best. You send him circling out of the backfield as a receiver. Whiz gets behind a linebacker. Tom Burns puts a pass right into his hands, and you've got 20 more yards.

The Gorillas get tough. With their fans yelling, "Dee-fense! Dee-fense!" they hold you to nine yards on the next three plays. You're on their 27-yard line now, with four minutes to go. Do you go for a first down, trying to keep driving for a touchdown that could win the game right now? Or do you try for a field goal that could send the game into overtime?

—To go for a first down, turn to page 55.

—To try a field goal, turn to page 56.

"Okay, Burns," you say. "Try it." He claps his hands and trots to the huddle.

At the line of scrimmage, Tiny Todd takes a step in, as if to block, then speeds to the goal line. Big Country Boone plunges into the line, as if he's carrying the ball. Tom Burns fakes a handoff, steps back and lofts a pass into the corner of the end zone. Without breaking stride, Tiny Todd hauls it in.

"Supermidget!" you scream. "Oh, you Supermidget!" That man may be only five-six, but his heart is as big as Clown Kennedy's helmet.

You win the game, and reporters say you're a genius for calling that play. But you know that all you did was trust your quarterback. For almost two full seasons Tom Burns said nothing. He sure picked the right time to speak up.

The End

Chub Kowalski comes in and kicks a field goal to tie the game. You go into overtime, but lose the coin toss, so the Gorillas receive. This is it. Time to play the toughest you ever have. The first team to score will win.

Your Hit Men do get tough. Their uniforms are stained with dirt. Their faces are crusty with dust and sweat. They ought to be exhausted, but they're not. No one can afford to get tired now.

(continued on page 45)

The Hit Men hold the Gorillas on three straight plays. Good work. Way to go. Now, the Gorillas must punt from their own 24-yard line. And you must make a decision.

The punt will probably come down around your own 40-yard line. Do you play it safe and have your players drop back on the punt to set up a regular return? Or do you send them charging through the line in an attempt to block the punt? They're all fired up now, after all. And any score will make you a winner—a field goal, a touchdown, or even a safety off a blocked punt.

—To try to block the punt, turn to page 60.

—To play it safe, turn to page 65.

You've got to do something to wake these bozos up. You've got to get the momentum back. You begin marching up and down the sidelines, slapping the helmets on your players' heads. You know that causes an awful ringing in their ears, but maybe they'll think they're hearing their alarm clocks and they'll wake up.

"Come on, you bozos," you yell. "Get going. Show me something. Where's your spirit? Where's your guts?"

You look around. "Who do I have here who can play some football?" you shout. "Who do I have here who can shake things up?"

Nobody says anything. Not even Clown Kennedy. And then, suddenly, someone springs to his feet and says, "I did' it before, coach, and I can do it now."

It's one of your reserve halfbacks, Fade-away Wallace. Four years ago, Wallace was Rookie-of-the-Year with Los Angeles. He had as great a season as Whiz Wilson is having for you now. He was known as Billy Wallace then. And he was famous for scoring touchdowns when his team needed them most.

(continued on page 47)

But after that great rookie season, he did nothing. He seemed to fumble whenever anyone tackled him. He dropped passes that were in his hands. He ended up on the bench and just faded out of the limelight. That's why he got his nickname, Fadeaway Wallace.

You took a chance on him this year, though. You signed him when Los Angeles released him. You had a feeling that he wanted to do well so badly that he'd be a good man for your suicide squad. And he has been. He's been a super hustler and a hard tackler. On kickoff returns, he's been a great blocker for Yo Yo Carpenter, too.

But you also had a feeling that maybe, some day, there'd be a time when he'd be able to reach back in the past and score a crucial touchdown for you. And here he is, Fadeaway Wallace, telling you that this is the time.

(continued on page 48)

You call for the trick play, the reverse on the kickoff return. "You're the key man," you tell Fadeaway. "Wake us up."

The Gorillas kick deep to Yo Yo Carpenter. Yo Yo catches the ball, races toward the right sideline and all the Gorillas run to that side, too, moving in on him. The Gorillas converge and, at the last moment, just as Yo Yo is about to be tackled, Fadeaway circles behind him, running toward the left sideline. Yo Yo hands the ball to him, and Fadeaway takes off. With a burst of speed from the old days, he races to the left sideline and cuts toward the goal line. The Gorillas have all been moving the other way. They can't recover in time to get him.

Only one man, the Gorilla kicker, has a chance to tackle Fadeaway. The kicker dives down low, trying to submarine him. Fadeaway hurdles over the kicker and flies to the end zone. He did it. He did what he said he would.

The touchdown fires up everybody. Your defense comes alive. So does your offense. Your hunch has paid off.

You win the game. And as far as you're concerned, from this moment on, Fadeaway Wallace ought to have a new nickname: The Comeback Kid.

The End

No need to get fancy, you decide. You've got five minutes on the clock and three time-outs. There's still time to try to get a good drive going. If you don't, then you can try some razzle-dazzle later.

Yo Yo Carpenter returns the Gorilla kick to your 33-yard line. Your line starts to do its job, opening holes for the runners and protecting the passer. Country Boone bangs off tackle for several gains. Whiz Wilson turns the corner for several more. Tom Burns completes short, sure passes to tight end Ed Rosen and flanker R. J. King. You're moving the ball and using up the clock expertly.

(continued on page 51)

With two minutes remaining in the game, you have a fourth down on the Gorilla 12-yard line. You send your kicking team onto the field. The score is tied, 17–17. A field goal will give you the lead.

Chub Kowalski kicks the ball straight over the crossbar and between the goal posts, putting you ahead, 20–17. Shaking his fist, all pumped up, he then booms the kickoff all the way out of the end zone. The Gorillas' great kick returner, Lucifer Brown, never gets a chance to even get his hands on the ball.

The Gorillas have the ball on their own 20-yard line. There are less than two minutes remaining. Should you stay in your regular defense? Or should you go to the "nickel defense," using five defensive backs instead of four? If you go to the nickel defense, you protect against long passes, but you'll be vulnerable to short stuff underneath and the Gorillas might be better able to drive close enough for a field goal to tie the game and send it into overtime.

—If you use the nickel defense, turn to page 61.

—If you use your regular defense, turn to page 68.

Delacruz is a little bit off stride. But he's able to get the punt away. It misses the coffin corner and bounces into the end zone. The Gorillas down it. They take over on their own 20-yard line.

This is the test you've been pointing toward all season. Close game. Last few minutes. Winner to go to the Super Bowl. This is what all those long practices were supposed to prepare you for. This is where the tougher team wins. You're happy you didn't try a fake punt. This is better. This is the fourth quarter, with the game on the line. This is what you like to call "Warrior time."

"Come on, you Hit Men," you holler out at the defense. "It's Warrior time, Warrior time."

Your bench picks up the yell: "Warrior time! Warrior time!" But the Gorilla fans are going berserk and The Zoo is so noisy that you can barely hear what your guys are saying. "No matter," you think. "The guys on the field *know* that it's Warrior time."

(continued on page 53)

They sure do. With Clown Kennedy and Hungry Hank leading them, The Hit Men hold the Gorillas on three straight plays. A Gorilla punt puts the ball on your 40-yard line. And now it's up to your offense. As Hungry Hank runs off the field, he passes Whiz Wilson. "Defense did it," Hank says. "Now it's Warrior time for the offense. You guys got to do it, too."

"Hungry Hank," says Whiz Wilson, "it's as good as done."

(continued on page 54)

Quarterback Burns begins moving the team downfield. He puts a bullet pass in Country Boone's belly for a first down. He pitches out to Whiz, who runs for another. He connects with R. J. King on a pass to the right sideline, and with Tiny Todd on a pass to the left sideline. "Warrior time!" you're hollering at the top of your lungs. "Warrior time!"

Oh, yes. How your team can play in the fourth quarter! That's what it's all about.

You're losing by four points, and the clock is winding down. Now you have the ball on the Gorillas' eight. And you know who you want to try to take it all the way in. Whiz Wilson. He's the man. You signal Tom Burns to give it to the Whiz.

Whiz Wilson doesn't let you down. He starts toward the middle, skips to the outside, then darts back inside. Moving every which way, he slithers through Gorilla tacklers. And into the end zone for the winning touchdown.

You didn't panic. You played your game. You had faith that the longer the game went on, the tougher your guys would be. And you can't wait for Warrior time in your next game—the Super Bowl.

The End

You're going to win it right now. You call for a double tight end, short-yardage formation, with Whiz Wilson taking one of his Wizard dives over the line of scrimmage. You watch the team line up, get set, snap the ball and block. You watch Whiz charge forward with the ball. And leap over the line. And come head to head with Killer Tedesco. You hear the crunch as they collide. And you know that you made a mistake. Whiz did not get the first down.

The Gorillas take over and use up the clock. You call all your time-outs but you can't slow down the game long enough to get the ball back. You lose, 10–7. You shouldn't have been greedy. You should have kicked the field goal to tie the game and taken your chances on winning it in overtime.

The End

"Kicking team," you call out. "Kicking team." You want the field goal to tie the game. You'll worry about winning it later.

Your place-kicker, Chub Kowalski, trots onto the field. Kowalski is one of those kickers who never looks up when he comes onto the field. He only looks at the ground. He doesn't look at the crowd. Or the scoreboard. Or other players. He doesn't even look at the goalposts. He lines up his kicks by looking at the hashmarks on the field. They are the same width as the goalposts and are in a direct line with the goalposts.

He does all this, Kowalski always says, because it helps him concentrate. By never looking up, he is able to keep his head down on the ball perfectly when he boots it. Also, he is never distracted by anything.

And that's important now. Because the Gorillas have Stretch Logan. Stretch is six-eight and a former college basketball star. When opponents try field goals, the Gorillas send in Stretch to jump up and down and wave his arms to distract the kicker. But since Chub Kowalski never looks up, Stretch can't bother him.

Chub was born in Poland. He played a lot of soccer there and that's how he developed a

(continued on page 57)

skill for kicking. Like so many pro kickers, he boots the ball with the side of his foot, soccer-style.

When he moved to the United States, he came here with an uncle. His parents remained in Poland. But they are here in the stadium today, on a visit to America. They've never seen a football game before. They don't know much about the rules. But you're sure that they know their son is in the limelight at this moment.

(continued on page 58)

R. J. King is the man who holds the ball for Chub. Since Chub never looks up from the ground, R. J. must mark the ball expertly for him. Now, R. J. shows Chub the spot on the 34-yard line where he's going to hold the ball, seven yards behind the line of scrimmage. Since the goalposts are ten yards deep in the end zone, the kick will have to travel 44 yards.

Arnie Hodge, the old veteran center, snaps the ball back. As Stretch Logan jumps and waves, R. J. places the ball down and Chub kicks it. The ball rockets into the air. It's straight on target. And it was kicked so hard that it would have been accurate from 54 yards. Chub Kowalski has come through again. This game is tied, 10–10.

Your defense holds the Gorillas. With one and a half minutes remaining in the game, you get the ball on your 42-yard line. You have two time-outs left.

Two passes and a run bring you a first down on the Gorilla 45, with 50 seconds to play. You call time out.

Back in action, Burns throws to Charlie Baggett for another first down. Then he throws a pass incomplete. On the second down, he fires to tight end Ed Rosen at the 30. And someone jumps in front of you, blocking your view.

(continued on page 59)

Angrily, you shove the person aside. You see Rosen holding the ball and struggling to try to get out of bounds to stop the clock. He can't make it. The clock is running and time is ticking away. There are 12 seconds remaining in the game. You have only one time-out left. What do you do? Do you call time out to kick the field goal right now? It would have to travel about 47 yards.

Or do you call your last time-out to set up one more passing play that might bring the ball in closer? You could complete a pass in five or six seconds and, if the receiver stepped out of bounds quickly to stop the clock, you'd have time enough for a field goal.

—If you want to kick the field goal now, turn to page 66.

—If you want to try one more pass first, turn to page 69.

The Warriors go full tilt for the block, every man but one charging through the line. And they crash into the punter a split second after he kicks the ball. It's a penalty—roughing the punter. And an automatic first down for the Gorillas.

That's just the break the Gorillas needed. With their fans almost tearing The Zoo apart, the Gorillas drive down and score a touchdown. They win the game, and the right to go to the Super Bowl.

It was Bobby Sam Smith who roughed the punter. But you can't be angry at him. It was your mistake that blew this game. You had no reason to block the punt. You should have been satisfied to get good field position and pound out yardage for a score.

The End

Frank Ellis sees that you're in the nickel defense. He knows that a quarterback always has to "take what you're giving him," which in this case means throwing short-yardage passes. He throws quick slants to his wide receivers and short bullets to his backs. But with time running against him, the best he can do is put the Gorillas on your 40-yard line, with a few seconds left. Their field-goal kicker has to boot it 57 yards, and his attempt sails wide to the left.

You leap high as time runs out. You've won the conference championship. You've beaten the Gorillas in their own Zoo.

The End

You can't risk your quarterback's getting hurt, so you call a safer play—a sweep by Whiz Wilson. Whiz picks up four yards, but then the Gorillas hold you on the next two plays. Faced with fourth down, you settle for a field goal. Chub Kowalski's kick puts you ahead, 3–0.

(continued on page 63)

In the second quarter, the Gorillas score a touchdown to take the lead, 7–3. They kick off. Yo Yo Carpenter catches the ball, is trapped on the three-yard line and fumbles. As the ball falls to the ground, you feel your heart pounding and your head grow tight with anger. "You fool," you yell. "That's why they call you Yo Yo." Carpenter dives on the ball, recovering his fumble, and you begin to breathe a little bit better.

But you're still in trouble. You're deep in your own territory—first down on the three.

You can't take any chances down here. So you call for a simple running play—fullback Country Boone up the middle. Whenever Country runs, he tucks the ball in very tightly. He's not a fumbler.

Country picks up one yard. You call the same play again and this time he's stopped for no gain. Third down coming up. You've got a decision to make.

(continued on page 64)

You've got to get out of trouble. You don't want to give the Gorillas terrific field position, but if you wait until fourth down to punt that's exactly what you'll do. Maybe you ought to surprise them with a quick kick—a punt on third down. Country Boone used to do some kicking in college, at Arkansas, and if he were able just to punt the ball over the heads of their defensive backs, it might roll into Gorilla territory.

However, pro teams almost never try quick kicks. That's something high schools and colleges do. The pros don't like to give up even one down. They always figure they can score on any play. So maybe you should wait until fourth down to punt. Maybe you should try a long pass. If Burns threw it very long—to the 50-yard line—you wouldn't be hurt too badly even if it were intercepted. As long as the man who intercepted it was tackled immediately.

—*If you call a quick kick, turn to page 72.*

—*If you call a long pass, turn to page 76.*

No sense in trying anything daring here. All you need is to make no mistakes and you'll have great field position. You see the punt go up and you're pleased when Charlie Baggett signals for a fair catch. He pulls in the ball safely on your 42-yard line.

You begin to move slowly, on short, careful sideline passes from Burns to the wide receivers. Then, with the Gorillas drifting out to protect the flanks, you have Country Boone drive up the middle for seven yards. Next, it's Whiz Wilson's turn. And the Whizzer does it for you again. "With the game on the line, the spotlight is mine," Whiz likes to say. And he's right. This time, he rolls around end for 26 yards, giving you a first down on the Gorillas' 12.

That's close enough. You send in Chub Kowalski right now. And Chub drills a field goal. You win in overtime by three points.

The End

You signal your team to let the clock run down to five seconds, then to call time out. The clock won't start again until the play gets under way, and since the play will take at least five seconds, the clock will run right out. That way, whether you make the field goal or miss it, the Gorillas will not get the ball again.

Chub Kowalski is going to have to kick it a long way. But he can do it. You know he can do it. He *has* to do it.

Nobody talks to him. They don't want to break his concentration. Chub walks around in small circles, looking at the ground. Circle after circle after circle, concentrating.

R. J. King points to the place where he'll spot the ball. Chub stares at it and says nothing. Across the line, the Gorillas are screaming at him. They're saying terrible things, trying to get Chub angry, trying to distract him.

It's time now. You clench your fists. You tug at your cap. You kick a clipboard that's lying at your feet.

(continued on page 67)

The ball is snapped. R. J. puts it down. The Gorillas' Stretch Logan leaps and waves. Chub steps forward, kicks, and . . .

. . . The ball flies high and deep, crosses the goal line and begins to wobble. You hold your breath. You wish you had a wind machine to give it some oomph. You watch and pray and, suddenly, you're cheering as loud as you ever have in your life. The ball has gone over for a field goal. The Warriors have won. Chub Kowalski is a great big hero and, as R. J. King and Arnie Hodge carry him off the field, you know that even though Chub's parents may not understand much about football, they sure understand what's happening right now.

The End

You are confident your defensive backs can handle the deep passing game and you see no reason to give away short yardage. Ellis, of course, picks up your defense instantly and goes deep. His pass is incomplete, but he's got you set up. As you think about long passes, he calls a draw play up the middle. It catches you completely by surprise and gains 35 yards.

Ellis fakes another run and cornerback Yo Yo Carpenter takes two steps up to stop it. This allows Gorilla receiver Elmers Kauffman to slip by him and break free. Your free safety, Ron Leonard, runs over to cover as Ellis fires long to Elmers. Leonard gets there just before the ball, but his momentum carries him into Kauffman for pass interference. This gives the Gorillas the ball on your two-yard line. Without even thinking of a field goal, they give the ball to their reliable fullback, Roger Walsh. As usual, Walsh storms for a gain behind the big Gorilla line. This gain is a big one. It carries him two yards into the end zone for the winning touchdown.

The End

During your time out, you tell Tom Burns to move the ball as close as he can to the end zone for the field goal attempt, but to be sure—before he throws it—that the receiver will be able to step out of bounds to stop the clock. "If there are any problems at all," you tell him, "be sure to throw the ball away, incomplete."

He nods. And when he gets back on the field everybody in the stadium knows what he's going to do. Tom fades to pass and spots R. J. King free at the right sideline. Tom fires and, suddenly, the Gorilla cornerback, Adams Elkins, steps out in front of R. J. Adams has been playing possum, making it seem as if R. J. were free. And his trickery works. Running full speed, he cuts off R. J. and intercepts the ball. Before you can even collect your thoughts, Adams is flying alone down the sideline for a touchdown.

You lose the game. And you deserve it. You should have tried a field goal right there. This was cutting it too close. You used your time out incorrectly.

The End

"Quarterback keeper. Take it yourself, Tom," you tell Tom Burns. "Put the ball in the end zone."

You step back and watch the play. Tom takes the snap, fakes to the fullback and hides the ball behind his hip. All the Gorilla linebackers go for the fake. All except one. As Burns slides down the line of scrimmage, trying to sneak around right end unnoticed, one Gorilla linebacker follows him all the way. The middle linebacker, Killer Tedesco.

Killer is keying on your quarterback, not letting him out of his sight. As Burns turns the corner, Killer is there. *Smash.* Killer hit Tom like a truck, driving Tom into the ground. Tom doesn't move. Killer has knocked him unconscious. You've lost Tom Burns for the rest of the game.

You never should have called that play this early in the game. You have lost your quarterback. And you end up losing the game. The Warrior offense is dead without Tom Burns. He has a concussion, and you have a headache, too.

The End

The Gorilla punter hangs a short kick high in the air. Charlie Baggett signals for a fair catch. The Gorilla punt-coverage team taunts him: "Afraid of us, gutless?" Charlie laughs.

The Gorillas stop you on three running plays, forcing you to punt with a little over three minutes to go. With Frank Ellis, their quarterback, mixing runs and passes, they drive to your four-yard line. Trailing by seven points, they need a touchdown. It's first down and goal to go, with 21 seconds remaining.

You put in your goal-line defense. On first down, Ellis's pass is incomplete. On second, there's an end run to your one-yard line. The Gorillas call time out, then Ellis is stopped on a quarterback sneak. Time is out again. This is it!

With four seconds left, Roger Walsh, the strapping fullback, gets the call. He dives up the middle. And Hungry Hank Hartman is there to meet him. Hank stops him short of the goal.

Your Hit Men have held. It was a great goal line stand. You win, 20–13. Your conservative strategy paid off—by a whisker.

The End

"Has Country been practicing his punting lately?" you ask one of your assistant coaches.

"Yeah, he boots a few every week," you're told.

That settles it, then. Quick kick. You send in the play.

Center Arnie Hodge snaps the ball between the legs of your quarterback, Tom Burns. It goes directly to Country, who's lined up five yards directly behind Burns. Country grabs the ball and kicks. It's a line-drive kick, barely clearing the heads of the linemen, but it picks up a little height, passes the defensive backs and rolls to the Gorilla 42. The Gorilla fans begin to taunt you: "High school play! High school play!" But you don't care. You fooled them and got out of trouble.

The Gorillas get going and score a field goal, moving ahead 10–3. But you come right back. With Whiz Wilson turning the ends, Country Boone pounding the middle and Tom Burns passing expertly, you drive to the Gorilla 36. You're rolling now.

(continued on page 73)

You call a running play to the left side of the field. Tom Burns pitches to Whiz Wilson. Whiz scampers wide for six yards. As Whiz runs left, something horrible happens on the other side of the field. While everybody is watching Whiz Wilson, Killer Tedesco takes a cheap shot at Tiny Todd Lewis. Killer wacks him across the head. Tiny Todd crumples to the ground in a daze.

(continued on page 74)

The Gorilla fans go wild. They begin thumping their chests. They throw bananas on the field. They stomp and cheer.

You are furious. And so are your players. You yell at the referee to call a penalty. But none of the officials saw Killer take the cheap shot.

You can't let Killer get away with this. He's been doing things like that all his career. The more he gets away with, the worse he gets. Pretty soon, opposing players begin thinking about him too much and don't concentrate on the game. Killer's intimidation has helped the Gorillas win a lot of games.

Well, he's not going to do that today. You won't let him. And neither will your players. "Send in The Hatchet," one of them yells.

"Yeah," yells another. "The Hatchet."

The Hatchet is just as mean as Killer. But The Hatchet is crazier. The Hatchet used to be an offensive tackle, but he grew so crazy and rough that he was always picking up penalties. You don't let him play on offense anymore. Not with that temper. You only let him play on the suicide squad.

(continued on page 75)

During the time out for Tiny Todd's injury, Arnie Hodge, your veteran center, runs over to you. "Coach," he says, "don't put Hatchet in. He'll just cost us. Let me handle Killer my way."

You look over at The Hatchet. He's got his helmet on and he's swinging his arms. He's hopping around, ready, eager. He wants the Killer. He wants to go out there and settle the score. And you know for sure he's one mean man who can do it. Arnie Hodge is tough, but not mean.

—*To put in The Hatchet, turn to page 79.*

—*To let Arnie Hodge try to handle Killer, turn to page 80.*

You send Tiny Todd Lewis, the super-midget, deep down the sidelines on a bomb. Quarterback Tom Burns drops four yards deep into the end zone, but the big Gorilla rush does not give him time to set up. Burns is being chased around. He scrambles toward the right side of the end zone with three Gorilla defensive linemen chasing him. He scrambles left. He can't allow himself to be tackled in the end zone or it will be a safety—two points for the Gorillas, plus possession of the ball.

Burns barely escapes the safety by diving out of the end zone. His forward progress carries him to the two-yard line. Now you have to send in your regular punting unit, and it will be cramped. Usually, the punter stands 15 yards back from the line of scrimmage. That way, he can take the snap, get a three-step approach and boot the ball away. But now, with only 12 yards to work with—the ten-yard end zone plus two yards of the field—you are worried that your punter, Martin Delacruz, might be in trouble.

(continued on page 77)

And you are right. The snap from center is high, and instead of having those extra three yards, which can often give you room to maneuver on a bad center snap, Delacruz is trapped. He leaps up and grabs the ball but can't retreat. He has no room. He tries to get a punt away, but it is blocked out of the end zone by the Gorillas. That, too, is a safety—just like having a player tackled in the end zone.

(continued on page 78)

The Gorillas go ahead, 9–3, and you have to kick or punt the ball to them from your own 20-yard line. You choose to have Delacruz punt the ball rather than have Chub Kowalski place-kick. A punt gets better hang time than a kick—stays in the air longer—and will give you more time to get downfield.

Delacruz gets off a poor punt. The Gorillas get excellent field position and score another touchdown, moving ahead 16–3. Your men are playing horribly. On offense, they are missing blocks and not picking up yards in the air or on the ground. On defense, they are lazy—arm-tackling rather than throwing their bodies around, and not rushing hard. As the first half ends, with your Warriors trailing 16–3, you follow the team into the locker room. What do you do? Do you yell at them to fire them up? What do you say? Maybe it's better to say nothing and hope they break out of the lazy spell on their own.

—If you decide to yell at the players, turn to page 83.

—If you decide to say nothing, turn to page 103.

You watch them carry Tiny Todd off the field. And you see the anger in Hatchet's eyes. "Hatchet," you yell. "Get in there."

He races onto the field, doing little leaps as he runs. On the first play, he races right at Killer Tedesco. As Tom Burns fires a 12-yard pass into Charlie Baggett's hands, Hatchet pounds Killer over the head with his right forearm pad and backhands him in the throat with his left arm. Then he knees Killer smack in the stomach.

Killer falls down. And the referee blows hard on his whistle.

The officials knew what Hatchet was going to do and were watching him the whole play. They throw Hatchet out of the game and hit your team with a penalty for unnecessary roughness. The completed pass doesn't count. Plus, you lose 15 yards, pushing you back to the 45.

The penalty stops your drive and you lose the momentum that you had before you let Killer Tedesco rile you into making a stupid substitution. You never get the momentum back. The Gorillas go on to win, 31–3.

The End

"Don't worry, Arnie," you tell your center. "I'm not letting the crazy man go in there. But we have to do something."

On the first play after that, Arnie Hodge does nothing. On the second play, he does nothing. On the third play, Tom Burns passes to R. J. King for a touchdown. And now everybody has forgotten about Killer's cheap shot.

The Warriors line up to kick the extra point. While everybody is watching kicker Chub Kowalski, Arnie Hodge sets his sights on Killer Tedesco. Hodge snaps the ball. Kowalski begins to kick. Killer jumps in the air to try to block it. And Arnie fires outright at Killer's knees. He crashes into those knees, catching Killer off balance, in mid-air.

Kowalski's kick goes through the uprights. Both teams run off the field. But one man stays behind. Killer Tedesco is on the ground, injured, holding his left knee.

Killer Tedesco has been knocked out of this game. And nobody saw Arnie Hodge do it.

(continued on page 81)

The first half ends with the score tied, 10–10. You receive the kickoff at the start of the second half, drive downfield and kick a field goal to go ahead, 13–10. A little while later, Clown Kennedy comes up to you. He says that the Gorilla right tackle, Les Rollins, is changing his stance slightly depending upon whether the Gorilla play is a pass or a run. From his position at defensive end, across the line from Rollins, Clown has watched this happen all game. He also spotted it during the week, he says, while looking at films of Gorilla games. By watching Les Rollins's stance, Clown says, he can tell in advance whether the Gorillas are going to pass or run.

(continued on page 82)

"Next time I spot a pass coming," says Clown, "let me use the special inside stunt pass rush."

You think about that for a moment. On the special inside stunt pass rush, Clown circles behind the defensive tackle, then rushes in from a surprising angle. It could work and get you a key sack. On the other hand, it could be very costly if Clown is wrong. Because by rushing in that way, Clown will leave a very big opening to the outside. And if the Gorillas have called a running play, not a pass, they could run to that spot for a very big gain.

—If you let Clown Kennedy call a special inside stunt pass rush, turn to page 87.

—If you tell him you don't want to take a chance on the stunt, turn to page 88.

"Warriors? You guys call yourself warriors?" you yell at your team. "You guys are out there like you are playing in a sandbox, not on a football field. The Super Bowl, gentlemen. This one is for the Super Bowl. How about a little enthusiasm out there?"

(continued on page 84)

All of a sudden, Hungry Hank Hartman leaps up and says, "Coach is right. Let's get out there and play these guys tough. Let's go to war and eat these Gorillas up! Come on!"

Arnie Hodge, the veteran center, steps to the front of the room. "I've been waiting for a Super Bowl all my life," he says. "I want that gold Super Bowl ring more than anything in the world right now. And I'm not gonna let any of you lazy jerks take it away from me. Anyone dogging it out there in the second half is gonna be running after the game. And I'm gonna be doing the chasing."

(continued on page 85)

Then Clown Kennedy speaks from his seat. "Eeek. Eeek. Eeek," he squeaks. "Are you gonna let them silly monkeys make you keep playing like mice?" he asks.

"No," yells the rest of the team.

"Who's gonna win, us or the chimpanzees?" Clown asks.

"We are," the team yells back.

Everybody starts chanting: "Super Bowl! Super Bowl! Super Bowl!"

They really want it now. You love it when your team leaders get everyone fired up like that. Your Warriors go bursting through the door, knocking each other over in their rush to get out on the field. Now the Warriors are ready to play. And you can start thinking about strategy.

(continued on page 86)

You consider making one technical adjustment for the second half. All first half Gorilla quarterback Frank Ellis picked your zone defense apart, throwing passes in the seams for short yardage and long drives. Should you stick with the zone? Or should you go to man-to-man coverage even though man-to-man is more susceptible to long passes? A breakdown in a zone might cost you 15 yards and a first down. A breakdown in man-to-man can cost you 60 yards and a touchdown.

—To switch to man-to-man coverage, turn to page 104.

—To remain in the zone defense, turn to page 108.

Clown is an old pro. He's been with you a long time. You trust his instincts and his intelligence. "Do it, Clown," you say. "But play it smart."

Clown tells left linebacker Abdul Amat what he's planning to do. That way, Abdul can cover for him a little bit on the outside. Then the next time Clown spots Rollins in the passing stance, he signals Abdul and begins the stunt. Slipping to the inside, Clown explodes through the line. Gorilla quarterback Frank Ellis is caught by surprise. Dropping back to pass, Ellis is popped by Clown before he even has time to set up. The ball rolls loose, the Warriors recover deep in Gorilla territory and go on to score a TD.

The Gorillas never are able to come back. Because of Clown's heads-up football, you win, 20–10.

The End

You tell Clown Kennedy that you don't think a stunt is worth the risk right now. And through the rest of the third quarter, your defense continues to play well without using it. But in the first minutes of the fourth quarter, the Gorillas get a field goal and tie the score, 13–13.

Now it's your turn. You get the ball on the kickoff and drive downfield. In all your crucial games this season, this has been when your Warriors have played best—in the fourth quarter, with the game on the line. Your fans call the fourth quarter "Warrior time."

(continued on page 89)

But the Gorillas are a tough fourth-quarter team, too. And after you drive to their 40-yard line, they stop you on two straight plays. There are nine minutes remaining in the game, you have a third down on their 38 and you need eight yards for a first down. It's clearly a passing down.

You think it's likely that the Gorillas will try a blitz—will shoot one of their linebackers in to try to get your quarterback. One way to beat a blitz is to call a draw play—a delayed handoff to a running back who races by the charging linebacker and into the hole the linebacker has left. But if the Gorillas don't blitz, there won't be a hole and it's very unlikely a draw will pick up the yardage you need for the first down. In that case, you'd be much better off trying a pass. What do you do?

—*If you decide to throw a pass, turn to page 90.*

—*If you guess blitz and call a draw play, turn to page 94.*

You call a ten-yard slant-out pass to tight end Ed Rosen. Big Ed. Ed was an All-America tackle in college—big, strong, good speed and an excellent blocker. But when your starting tight end got hurt at the beginning of training camp two years ago, and you couldn't trade for another you really liked, you switched Ed's position. You were deep in talent at tackle and you could afford to do that. You had a hunch Ed would be great at the new position. Since a tight end's main responsibility in your offense is to block, you were willing to sacrifice Ed's lack of pass-catching experience for his good blocking. And you knew that, at 6–6, with his speed and soft hands, Ed had the natural tools of a splendid receiver. You were putting together a team for the future. You could give him some time to develop.

(continued on page 91)

At first, Ed didn't like the idea. "I like it on the line, in the trenches," he told you. "I'm not a glamour-boy receiver."

But he went along with your plan, anyway. He had no choice. And he worked hard. During this last off-season, he would go down to a local high school every day, with a sack of balls, and have whomever was around throw passes to him until his hands got sore. The hard work paid off. This year, in addition to being a great blocker, Ed has sure hands. He's the guy you like to throw to when you need a key first down.

And right now you need one.

(continued on page 93)

Tom Burns scans the defense. No blitz seems to be coming. He drops back and fires low to Big Ed on the sidelines. It's a pass that Ed never would have caught last year—down around his ankles. But this year is different. He drops to one knee and cradles the ball to his chest. First down.

Three downs later, Whiz Wilson breaks wide for a touchdown and you lead, 20–13. You hold on to that lead and with five minutes left in the game the Gorillas are set to punt to you from their own 35. You must decide whether to sit on your lead or whether to keep trying to enlarge it. If you want to sit on the lead, you'll have to tell the punt-returner that, no matter what, he should call for a fair catch. If you want to play for more points, you'll tell him to run the punt back if he thinks there's a chance for a good return.

—If you want a fair catch, turn to page 71.

—If you want to give him the okay to return the punt, turn to page 97.

This seems like such an obvious blitzing situation that you decide to outsmart the Gorillas by calling a draw. "Pro set, halfback draw left" is the play you send into the game. That's Whiz Wilson on a delayed handoff to the left side of the center.

Quarterback Tom Burns takes the snap and moves back as if he's going to pass. Instead, he sticks the ball into Wilson's belly. Whiz races toward the line of scrimmage, but there are no holes. The Gorillas have not called a blitz. Whiz runs smack into a line of tacklers. No gain.

(continued on page 95)

And, even worse, in the pileup Whiz sprains his ankle. He has to come out of the game. Here you are, with the score tied in the middle of the fourth quarter, and you're without both your top running back, Whiz Wilson, and your swiftest wide receiver, Tiny Todd Lewis.

When you get the ball back, who will you put in to replace Whiz? There's that rookie, Tony Vincent, who has breakaway speed and is always a touchdown threat. But he's never played in such an important game. He will definitely be nervous and he has a tendency to fumble, anyway.

(continued on page 96)

But if not Tony Vincent, who? Because of an injury this week in practice, your number-one reserve halfback isn't available. The only other halfback you have available today is Fadeaway Wallace. Once, Fadeaway was a great running back. But in the past few years he has lost it all. You have him on your team because he's a great hustler, always trying hard. He's a good influence on other players. Also, he's got the speed and the guts to get downfield fast to make tackles for the suicide squad.

But as a running back? All Fadeaway has to recommend him for that is his experience. And the fact that a few years ago he was as tough to tackle as a ghost.

—To put in Tony Vincent, turn to page 98.

—To put in Fadeaway Wallace, turn to page 100.

"Don't let up," you tell your players before the punt. You know that when teams sit on leads, they sometimes get complacent and blow games. Since Charlie Baggett doesn't fumble many returns, you decide to let him run back the punt and keep the pressure on the Gorillas.

Charlie picks up seven yards on the return. But more important than the yards, his return lets the Gorillas know that you're not going to take it easy, that you're going to keep pouring it on.

Your offense marches downfield, eating up the clock. And what's more, you score an insurance touchdown. The Gorillas are caged.

When the gun goes off, you're ahead, 27–13. Next stop, the Super Bowl.

The End

You get back the ball with four and a half minutes left. The score is still tied at 13. "Vincent," you say, "get in there." You're not very happy about it, but you keep telling yourself, "Any time he gets his hands on the ball, he's capable of breaking away for a score."

Your offense can't get moving. And Burns is sacked on third down when Vincent misses a block.

But your All-Pro safety, Ron Leonard, intercepts a pass. You've got another chance with two minutes left in the game.

The ball is on your own 28-yard line. You decide you'll try to get Vincent the ball in the open field, where he can use his speed. First, you send him on a sweep, but it doesn't work. Then you decide on a swing pass. That will isolate him one-on-one with a linebacker, and there's no linebacker in the league who can keep up with Tony Vincent if it comes down to a foot race.

(continued on page 99)

Quarterback Burns drops back and throws to Vincent in the flat. Vincent reaches for the ball, gets his hands on it and takes off upfield as fast as he can move. Except he forgot something. The ball. The rookie ran before he had secure possession of the ball. He's now ten yards away from where the ball is bouncing on the ground.

It looked to you like an incomplete pass. But the officials rule it a fumble. The Gorillas recover the ball and kick a field goal with 23 seconds remaining. You lose, 16–13.

The End

Your defense forces the Gorillas to punt with four and a half minutes left in the game. You look down the bench. There's number 42, Fadeaway Wallace. That number brings back memories. Memories of the year he was the best back in the league. Memories of how he slashed, hurdled, dove and even passed for TD's. How you wish that just for the rest of this fourth quarter, just for four and a half minutes, Fadeaway Wallace could fade back again.

"Well, there's only one way to find out," you mutter to yourself. At the top of your lungs, you bellow, "Forty-two! Over here!" Fadeaway trots over. "Just like the old days," you tell him. "Let's win this one."

Fadeaway cracks a little smile and jogs onto the field. He throws a great block, which allows Tom Burns to complete a pass to the Warrior 42. Later, Fadeaway picks up six yards on a sweep.

You notice something on the sweep that gives you an idea. The Gorilla cornerback is accustomed to containing Whiz Wilson, so he comes up hard as soon as he sees a sweep coming. If he plays that way against Fadeaway, Fadeaway can do something that Whiz can't: Fadeaway can throw a halfback option pass.

(continued on page 101)

It's third and two on the Gorilla 30, with one minute and forty-five seconds left. You call the same sweep as before, but this time you tell wide receiver R. J. King to slip into the end zone behind the cornerback and you tell Fadeaway to throw the ball if R. J. is open.

Fadeaway takes the pitchout, the cornerback comes up on the play and R. J. sneaks behind him. Fadeaway lofts a wobbly pass toward the goal line.

(continued on page 102)

All alone in the end zone, R. J. King reaches out. And makes the catch. Touchdown.

The pass wins the game. Putting Fadeaway in added a whole new dimension to your offense. It gave you a chance to call a play the Gorillas were not prepared for. What a great decision. What a great way to end the game. "We couldn't have done that," you tell Wallace in the locker room, "with Whiz in there."

Then Whiz comes hobbling over. "You're not better than me," Whiz tells Wallace, "because nobody is. But," Whiz Wilson says, hugging his teammate, "you sure are the second best."

The End

You just don't know what to say to them. You've never seen your team this sluggish before. Your guys are playing like they don't want to win. They're sitting around the locker room, chewing on oranges and drinking Gatorade, and you are so disgusted you don't want to say anything to them. If they don't want to go to the Super Bowl, you tell yourself, then you don't want to, either. They've all given up. You can tell by the looks on their faces. And in the second half they get blown out just like in the first half, and they lose by 30 points.

Your team gave up after the first half of play. And you gave up, too. You should have been talking in that locker room, stirring up emotions, trying to get something going. You are all a bunch of quitters. The Warriors don't belong in the Super Bowl and they are not going there.

The End

That surge of determination as the Warriors bolted to the field gave you renewed confidence in your team. You have faith once again in your players' ability to perform. Why not go man-to-man with the Gorillas? As far as you're concerned, you have better men.

You are worried about only one match-up: Nathaniel Busby, your right cornerback, against the Gorillas' super wide receiver, El- mers Kauffman.

Elmers has good speed and great hands. He catches passes as if they were glued to his hands. And he is a little quicker than Nathaniel.

But Nathaniel is a smart cornerback. He reads receivers' eyes well and is rarely fooled by a stutter step or by a fancy move. His father was a defensive back with the old Cleveland Browns and New York Giants but never won a championship game. Nathaniel has inherited his father's defensive back instincts. But you hope he does not have his father's champion- ship-game jinx.

(continued on page 105)

The Gorillas are forced to punt on their first possession. But soon their veteran quarterback, Frank Ellis, adapts to the man-to-man coverage and completes some quick passes to Elmers Kauffman. Nathaniel is giving Elmers enough trouble, however, to prevent any real damage.

Your Warriors score a touchdown with ten minutes left in the game. Midway through the fourth quarter, they are trailing 16–10. With six minutes to go, the Gorillas have the ball, third and seven, on their own 32-yard line. You look up and see your All-Pro free safety, Ron Leonard, talking to Nathaniel. They both know that Ellis likes to throw to Elmers in these tough third-down situations and they are conceiving their strategy for the play.

(continued on page 106)

Ellis goes back to pass, scans the field and spots Elmers, who appears to be open. Ellis fires a pass to Elmers. This is exactly what Nathaniel and Ron have plotted. Nathaniel has been giving Elmers room, so he would seem open. Ron has been decoying, standing about five yards away.

The instant Ellis releases the ball, Ron dashes in front of Elmers to make an interception. Ron races upfield with the ball. At the Gorilla 35, he's about to be tackled by the big fullback, Roger Walsh. Juking and faking as Walsh dives in, Ron spots Nathaniel coming up behind him. Walsh blasts into Ron's legs and Ron laterals the ball to Nathaniel. As Ron is pounded to the ground, Nathaniel bolts for a touchdown.

The touchdown and extra point put you ahead, 17–16, and that's the way the game ends. Nathaniel's father comes down to the locker room, smiling with pride. He never won a championship, but his son just did. Nathaniel Busby is going to the Super Bowl. And so are you. You're going because of your decision to play man-to-man defense in the second half. The winning interception-touchdown came on a free-lance play that could not have been executed under a strict zone.

The End

When you went into the locker room at half-time, you thought you'd have to make a big change in your defensive pass coverage. Now, after observing your players' sudden spirit, you decide that your strategy wasn't at fault. The problem was not that you were using zone coverage, but that your players weren't alive and alert, and they were not executing properly. They seem alive and determined now. So you decide that the zone will work.

You are right. The Warriors receive the kick-off, drive downfield and Whiz Wilson breaks around left end, juking, slipping and sliding off tacklers for an eight-yard touchdown. Chub Kowalski adds the extra point and you are trailing by six, 16–10. While Whiz is waving to the CBS TV cameras and mouthing, "Hi, Mom" to his mother back home, your defense is shutting down the Gorillas. Wow! What a change from the first half. The Hit Men are hitting again. The Warriors are playing again.

(continued on page 109)

Late in the fourth quarter, with four minutes to go, you are still behind 16–10. It's the Gorillas' ball, third and six, from their own 22-yard line. Frank Ellis drops back, sets and tosses incomplete to Elmers Kauffman. Fourth down. The Gorillas have to punt.

But wait. There was a flag on the play. "The penalty better not be against us," you think.

It isn't. A Gorilla was caught holding on the pass play. Ten yard penalty. You have the option to accept or decline the penalty. If you decline, the Gorillas punt right now, from their 22. If you accept, the line of scrimmage will be moved back ten yards and the Gorillas will play third down over again.

—To accept the penalty, turn to page 110.

—To decline the penalty, turn to page 112.

110 _____

In the stands the Gorilla fans are going bananas. They are booing the officials, stomping in the aisles, screaming their stupid heads off. You can't quite figure out why they're so upset. After all, it wasn't as if the penalty had taken away a big gain—or any gain at all, for that matter. The pass had been incomplete.

But who knows why Gorilla fans do anything? They're simply nuts, that's all. And you can't be concerned about them. You have to decide what to do.

As two fans in gorilla costumes run out on the field, you shout instructions to your defensive captain, Hungry Hank Hartman. "Take it, Hank," you say. He tells the officials that the Warriors accept the penalty.

Okay. That pushes the Gorillas back to their 12-yard line. You assume they will try a safe run, which you can stop easily. Then they will be forced to punt from even deeper in their own territory than if you had declined the penalty. That will mean better field position for you on what may be your final drive.

(continued on page 111)

When Gorilla quarterback Frank Ellis learns you are taking the penalty, he looks a little surprised. And he does not call a run. He takes another chance to go for the first down.

Ellis fakes a handoff to his halfback, then sprints out to his right and fires another pass to Elmers Kauffman. This time it is complete for a first down.

The Gorillas march down to score a touchdown and win the game, 23–10. You never should have given Frank Ellis a second chance.

The End

"We don't want it," you yell to your defensive captain, Hungry Hank Hartman. "We decline." No way are you going to give Frank Ellis a second chance. What you need now are points. And you can't score without the ball.

Charlie Baggett catches the Gorilla punt on the Warriors' 45-yard line and returns it six yards to the Gorilla 49. There are three minutes and forty-three seconds remaining; plenty of time to score. You mix some safe runs and short passes and move the ball to the Gorilla 27-yard line. It's fourth down and one yard to go for a first down, with two minutes and twenty seconds left in the game. "Gotta go for it," you decide. You're a little too far for a sure field goal and you do need seven points to win.

Usually, you give the ball to Country Boone, the fullback, in short yardage situations. But the Gorillas will be expecting him. And Whiz Wilson loves to perform under pressure. You call for a fake to Country and a handoff to Whiz.

Whiz takes the handoff and hurdles for the first down. A minute later the offense is stopped again. Fourth and nine at the Gorilla 14-yard line.

(continued on page 113)

This time you decide to take the field goal. Chub Kowalski boots it perfectly. You trail, 16–13, with a little more than a minute to go. You have three time-outs remaining. What should you do on the kickoff? Should you attempt an onside kick—squirt the ball ten yards and try to recover it? Or should you kick deep and hope that a combination of tough defense and your three time-outs can get the ball back in time to score more points?

—*To kick deep, turn to page 114.*

—*For an onside kick, turn to page 116.*

You know that the Gorillas need only five plays to run out the clock, but you are confident your Hit Men can stop them and get the ball back for your offense. There's also a chance that your great suicide squad can cause a fumble on the kickoff.

That doesn't happen as the Gorillas safely return Kowalski's kick to their 24-yard line. The clock stops with one minute eight seconds remaining in the game. This is Warrior time.

(continued on page 115)

Both teams know what the Gorillas will call: Straight handoffs to their sure-handed fullback Roger Walsh. The only question is: Who is stronger, your defensive line or their offensive line? This is what those long practices were all about.

On first down, Clown Kennedy stops Walsh after one yard. Time out. Second down, Walsh picks up six. Time out again. Third down and three, with 51 seconds left. This is it. Stop them here and you get the ball back. Don't stop them and you lose.

Walsh bulls right up the middle and faces a head-to-head confrontation with Hungry Hank. Hank stands Walsh up for a split second. But no other Warriors converge to help out on the tackle. Walsh falls forward.

Is it a first down? It's going to be close. The officials bring the chains onto the field for a measurement. The chains are pulled taut. The referee looks closely and then signals. . . .

You know the decision before he signals. You can tell because, simultaneously, Hungry Hank throws his helmet down in disgust and Frank Ellis raises his arms in victory.

First down. You lose.

The End

This is no time to monkey around on defense. You need the ball. You've got to try an onside kick.

For you to get possession, the kickoff has to roll ten yards before the kicking team recovers it. You tell Chub Kowalski to tee up the ball on its side and kick a high, hopping groundball. You take out your regular suicide squad players and put in all your receivers, running backs and defensive backs—the guys with the best hands on the team. Nathaniel Busby is in. And Ron Leonard. And Whiz Wilson.

Kowalski kicks from your 35-yard line. The ball skips, hops, squibs and then shoots into the air. Stumbling at midfield, Whiz Wilson reaches down, snatches the ball and falls on it.

You recovered. There are 63 seconds left. A field goal will send the game into overtime. A touchdown will send you to the Super Bowl.

Burns throws to Ed Rosen for eight yards. Whiz takes a draw up the middle for 14. Tiny Todd Lewis, the Supermidget, gains seven on a reverse. With the clock ticking down to 30 seconds, you have the ball on the Gorilla 21-yard line.

(continued on page 117)

You call a sweep: Whiz Wilson following Curly Johanson to the wide side of the field. "You and me, Curly," Whiz says in the huddle. "We're goin' for a stroll. A stroll down Victory Lane."

(continued on page 118)

Quarterback Burns pitches to Whiz, who sprints right, dashes outside a block by Curly, cuts inside and dances back to the sideline. Whiz turns the corner and he's gone. Twenty-one yards. A touchdown.

Chub Kowalski makes the conversion and the Warriors win, 20–16. The team carries you and Whiz into the locker room. You sit there, already thinking about strategy for the Super Bowl, when you overhear Whiz doing a post-game interview. "I do it all," you hear Whiz telling a sportswriter. "Run, pass, punt. Nothing I can't do. Just watch me in the Super Bowl. This one was just the warm-up. That one's gonna be the real show."

You listen and laugh. You sure hope so. You sure hope he's right. Whiz Wilson has a big mouth. But it's nowhere near as big as his heart.

The End

ABOUT THE AUTHOR
& ILLUSTRATOR

Following their championship season in 1977, MITCH GELMAN's high school football coach, Glenn Bell, described him to a Los Angeles sports columnist as "the smartest quarterback I've ever coached." Mitch has brought his football knowledge from the playing field to the pages of this, his third book. Currently a senior at the University of California at Berkeley, Mitch is also the author of *Great Quarterbacks of Pro Football* and *Can You Win the Pennant? A Play It Your Way Sports Book #1*. He has worked as a reporter for *Time* magazine and the Los Angeles *Herald-Examiner*.

With thirty years of experience behind him, AL FIORENTINO is a very versatile artist. After graduating from the Philadelphia College of Art, he worked as an advertising illustrator. Since then he has also worked in book illustration and painting. Rather than limiting himself to a specific area, he enjoys doing everything from portraits and landscapes to animals and sports players! Mr. Fiorentino's studio is located in Yardley, Pennsylvania, and he lives nearby with his wife, who is an art teacher.